A Note to Parents

Dorling Kindersley Readers is a compelling program for beginning readers, designed in conjunction with leading literacy experts, including Dr. Linda Gambrell, Director of the School of Education at Clemson University. Dr. Gambrell has served on the Board of Directors of the International Reading Association and as President of the National Reading Conference.

Beautiful illustrations and superb full-color photographs combine with engaging, easy-to-read stories to offer a fresh approach to each subject in the series. Each *Dorling Kindersley Reader* is guaranteed to capture a child's interest while developing his or her reading skills, general knowledge, and love of reading.

The four levels of *Dorling Kindersley Readers* are aimed at different reading abilities, enabling you to choose the books that are exactly right for your child:

Level 1 – Beginning to read
Level 2 – Beginning to read alone
Level 3 – Reading alone
Level 4 – Proficient readers

The "normal" age at which a child begins to read can be anywhere from three to eight years old, so these levels are intended only a general guideline.

No matter which level you select, you can be sure that you are helping your child learn to read, then read to learn!

Dorling **DK** Kindersley

LONDON, NEW YORK, SYDNEY, DELHI, PARIS,
MUNICH, and JOHANNESBURG

Project Editor Naia Bray-Moffatt
Art Editor Catherine Goldsmith
Senior Art Editor Clare Shedden
Series Editor Deborah Lock
US Editor Adrienne Betz
Production Shivani Pandey
Jacket Designer Sophia Tampakopoulos
Photographer Andy Crawford

Reading Consultant
Linda Gambrell, Ph.D.

First American Edition, 2001
00 01 02 03 04 05 10 9 8 7 6 5 4 3 2 1
Published in the United States by DK Publishing, Inc.
95 Madison Avenue, New York, New York 10016

Published in Great Britain by Dorling Kindersley Limited.

A Cataloging-in-Publication record is available
from the Library of Congress.

ISBN 0-7894-7875-7 (plc) 0-7894-7876-5 (pb)

Color reproduction by Colourscan, Singapore
Printed and bound in China by L Rex Printing Co., Ltd.

The publisher would like to thank the following:

Models: Philippa Parsons, Jo Parsons, Clifford Parsons,
Harriet Parsons, Timothy Parsons, Hannah Golding
and Mark the cat.

see our complete
catalog at
www.dk.com

DK DORLING KINDERSLEY *READERS*

BEGINNING **1** TO READ

My Cat's Secret

Written by Karen Wallace

DK

A Dorling Kindersley Book

Sarah was a girl
who loved cats.

cat

She loved big cats . . .

and little cats.

She loved long-haired
fluffy cats . . .

and short-haired
silky cats.

She loved black cats
with yellow eyes . . .

and gray cats
with blue eyes.

But Sarah did not have a cat.
Pets were not allowed
where she lived.

Then one day
Sarah's Mom and Dad
had exciting news.

"We're moving," Mom said.
"You will have your own room
and a yard to play in."

"Can I have a cat?" asked Sarah.

Dad smiled.
"Wait and see," he said.

Two weeks later, Sarah moved into her new house.

While Mom and Dad
unpacked the boxes,
Sarah sorted out her bedroom.
Then she went downstairs.

There was a box
on the kitchen floor.
It had holes in one end
and a handle on the top.

"Open it!"
said Dad with a smile.

Sarah bent down
and opened the box.

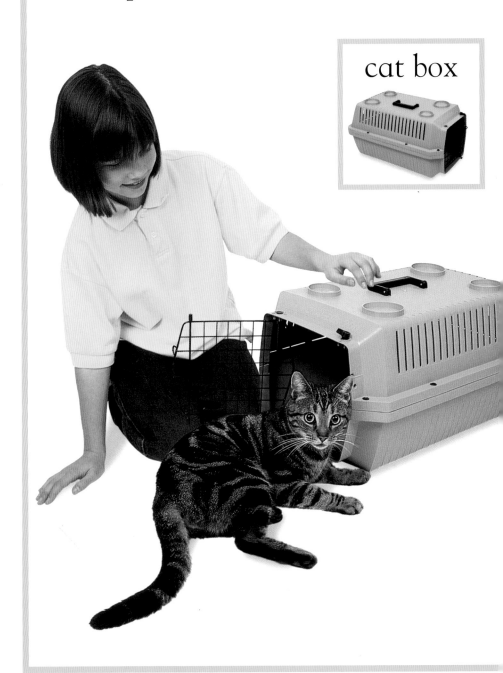

cat box

Inside was a
lovely little cat.
Her fur was stripy
and soft.

"Her name is Tabby," said Dad.
"She belonged to the people
who lived here before us."

"Can we keep her?" asked Sarah.

"Of course," said Dad.

Tabby had two bowls.
One was for her food.
The other was for her water.

"She needs to eat once a day,"
said Mom.
"She also needs fresh water
in her bowl."

cat flap

Mom put
a new cat flap
in the back door.
Now Tabby could go outside
whenever she wanted.

The next day, Mom and Sarah took Tabby to the vet.

The vet looked in Tabby's ears. Then she felt the cat's tummy.

"Is something wrong with Tabby?" Sarah asked.

The vet shook her head. "Don't worry," she said. "Your cat is very healthy."

"All cats should have a check-up from time to time," said Mom.

vet

All summer long
Sarah and Tabby played together.
On sunny days,
they played in the yard.

On rainy days,
Sarah made balls out of yarn
and Tabby chased after them.

ball

But Sarah and Tabby
were not always together.
Sometimes, Sarah liked to play
with her friends.

Tabby liked to go out
and play with her friends, too.

One night,
Sarah had a bad dream.

"I dreamed that Tabby
got stuck in a hole," said Sarah.

"Cats are very careful,"
Mom said gently.
"If their whiskers
touch the sides of a space,
they won't crawl in."

whiskers

One day Sarah noticed that
Tabby was getting fatter.
She was always lying down, too.

Sarah tickled Tabby's ears.
The cat purred
and blinked her eyes.
It was as if she had a secret
she was keeping to herself.

On Sarah's birthday,
Mom made her
a special birthday cake
in the shape of a cat.

Dad gave Sarah a necklace
with a cat on it.
"Oh thank you," Sarah cried.
"I must show Tabby."

cat
basket

Mom and Sarah
looked and looked for Tabby.
They looked in her favorite chair
and in her cat basket.

Then they looked in the yard.

They could not find her anywhere.
"I have a cat necklace
and a cat cake," Sarah cried.
"But no cat! Tabby has gone!"

At that moment,
Dad rushed into
the kitchen.

"Follow me!" he cried.
"I have a surprise for you."

"Have you found Tabby?"
asked Sarah.

"You'll see!" cried Dad.
"Look in your bedroom!"

Sarah ran up the stairs
and raced into
her bedroom.

The bottom drawer
was open.

Tabby was inside.
Two tiny kittens
were curled up
beside her.

Tabby looked up
and blinked.
"Happy birthday,"
she seemed to say.

Sarah looked down at the kittens.
They were the most
purr-r-fect presents, ever!

kittens

Picture word list

 cat

page 4

 ball

page 17

 cat box

page 10

 whiskers

page 21

 cat flap

page 13

 cat basket

page 26

 vet

page 15

 kittens

page 31

32